Caroline Quarlls AND THE
UNDERGROUND RAILROAD

Other Badger Biographies

Caroline Quarlls AND THE UNDERGROUND RAILROAD

JULIA PFERDEHIRT

Wisconsin Historical Society Press

Published by the Wisconsin Historical Society Press
Publishers since 1855

© 2008 by State Historical Society of Wisconsin

Publication of this book was made possible, in part, by gifts from the following donors:
Mrs. Harvey E. Vick of Milwaukee, Wisconsin
Helen Bader Foundation, Inc.

wisconsinhistory.org

Photographs identified with PH, WHi, or WHS are from the Society's collections; address inquiries about such photos to the Visual Materials Archivist at the above address.

Printed in the United States of America
Designed by Mark Skowron / Composure Graphics

13 12 11 10 09   2 3 4 5 6

Library of Congress Cataloging-in-Publication Data

Pferdehirt, Julia, 1952–
    Caroline Quarlls and the Underground Railroad / Julia Pferdehirt.
        p. cm. — (Badger biographies)
    Includes bibliographical references and index.
        ISBN 978-0-87020-388-6 (pbk. : alk. paper)
1. Quarlls, Caroline, b. 1826—Juvenile literature. 2. Fugitive slaves—United States—Biography—Juvenile literature. 3. Slaves—Missouri—Saint Louis—Biography—Juvenile literature. 4. Women slaves—Missouri—Saint Louis—Biography—Juvenile literature. 5. African American women—Missouri—Saint Louis—Biography—Juvenile literature. 6. Underground Railroad—Illinois—Juvenile literature. 7. Underground Railroad—Wisconsin—Juvenile literature. 8. Saint Louis (Mo.)—Biography—Juvenile literature. I. Title.
    E450.Q37P48 2008
    973.7'115092—dc22—
    [B]

                                    2007037331

Front cover: artist Jerry Butler
Back cover: WHi Image ID 52619

∞ The paper used in this publication meets the minimum requirements of the American National Standard for Information Sciences—Permanence of Paper for Printed Library Materials, ANSI Z39.48–1992.

This book is dedicated to my daughters,
Beth Aceituno, Becky Pferdehirt, and Ruth Pferdehirt—
a story of a young woman's dream dedicated to
three beautiful women with dreams of their own.

Contents

1

Meet Caroline Quarlls

In 1826, Caroline Quarlls was born in Missouri. Her mother was a slave, so Caroline would grow up in slavery. By this time, slavery had been allowed in the United States for more than 200 years. Millions of people had spent their whole lives as slaves. At first, most states allowed slavery. Then, one by one, states in the North passed laws against it. By the time Caroline was born, only Southern states allowed slavery. Northern states didn't.

Abolitionists gathered at conventions like the one advertised in this poster to discuss their antislavery views.

Some people were for slavery and others were against it. The country was beginning to divide in half. But, in the North and the South, a few people called **abolitionists** were working to end slavery everywhere.

abolitionist: (ab uh **lish** un nist) a person who is against slavery

1

Some abolitionists helped people escape from slavery to freedom in Northern states and Canada. These abolitionists, and the people they helped, are now known as the Underground Railroad.

This is Caroline's story. The story of one young woman who escaped from slavery. She dreamed of freedom and risked everything to make that dream come true.

What's in a Name?

Part of the mystery and fun of historical research is asking questions and discovering new answers. This was the case with Caroline's last name. When you read other books about Caroline, you might encounter different spellings of her last name. That is because in the process of writing down histories, information is sometimes understood differently by different people. In this book, we use "Quarlls" because that is the spelling that Caroline used in her own writings and because her family members use that spelling.

2

Independence Day

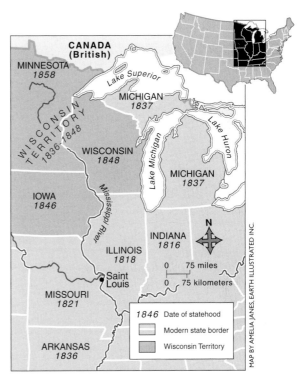

It was July 4, 1842. Independence Day. While the people of St. Louis, Missouri, celebrated with parades and picnics, Caroline Quarlls celebrated in a different way. Carrying everything she owned—$100, some clothes, and some jewelry—she declared her own independence. She ran away from slavery to freedom.

Caroline was living in St. Louis, Missouri, when she ran away.

Caroline's father was Robert Pryor Quarlls, a slave owner.
When he died, his **will** said Caroline would be given to
his sister, Mrs. Charles Hall. Mrs. Hall became Caroline's
"mistress," and she became Mrs. Hall's property.

Caroline grew into a slender, dark-haired girl. In 1842, she
was 16. Like every slave, she worked hard. When Mrs. Hall
wanted lace, Caroline sewed. When Mrs. Hall had guests,
Caroline waited on them. Every Sunday, Caroline and the
other house servants were locked in the house while Mr. and
Mrs. Hall went to the Presbyterian Church in St. Louis. While
the owners listened to their preacher, Caroline "scrubbed
paints"—that is, she washed wooden floors—in the Halls' big,
beautiful house.

Caroline wanted to be free. She thought about freedom,
although she'd never seen freedom. She'd never felt freedom.
But Caroline knew she wanted freedom!

Caroline's mother and sister died. But she wasn't totally
alone. She had a grandmother and stepfather. Her stepfather
was a free black man. No one knows today whether he was

will: written instructions that tell what should be done with someone's property and money when that person dies

born of free parents or whether he'd bought his freedom. He worked as a **blacksmith** and even made silver jewelry for Caroline.

A blacksmith at work

One day, for some long-forgotten reason—or maybe no reason at all—Mrs. Hall was angry. She was so angry she grabbed Caroline's long, curly hair. She snatched a pair of scissors and cut until a pile of dark curls lay on the floor. Caroline couldn't call for help. She couldn't fight. Who would take her side? No one. She was a slave, and Mrs. Hall could do whatever she wanted.

On that day, Caroline decided to run away. She had listened to every word about freedom and the North. She gathered clothes and a box for traveling. Somehow she "came by" $100. Later, some people said she'd been given the money. Others said she earned it by sewing. Perhaps she took the money from her master, Mr. Hall.

blacksmith: someone who makes and fits horseshoes and mends things made of iron

Many years later, Caroline wrote, "I told my grandmother that I was going to Canada but I was so young that she did not pay any attention to me…." So Caroline made her plans alone. She remembered that when she was ready, "I got the box out of my master's storeroom and hid it in a cherry hedge. I left on the 4th of July." She had big plans for a 16-year-old girl.

Caroline had planned carefully. She begged Mrs. Hall for permission to visit a sick friend. Then, she carefully packed the money, her clothes, and her silver jewelry. Caroline *did* make a quick visit to her friend. But it wasn't just to say, "Get well." She said, "Good-bye." Forever.

Mrs. Hall thought Caroline was still visiting her friend. Instead, Caroline snatched her precious box from under the cherry hedge and headed toward downtown St. Louis and

St. Louis viewed from the Mississippi River, around 1855

the **harbor** along the Mississippi River. It was 5:00 in the afternoon. There was no time to waste. Soon, the steamboat would be leaving for Illinois.

At this moment, Caroline used the only gift her father had ever given her—the color of her skin. Robert Quarlls had never taken care of her. But, because his skin was white, Caroline's skin color was very light. That day, Caroline hoped everyone would believe she was white, too.

Steamboat on the Mississippi River

harbor (**har** bur): a place where boats stop or unload their goods

7

Caroline bought a ticket to travel across the Mississippi River to Alton, Illinois. Alton wasn't far away. But, for Caroline, it was another world. In St. Louis, Caroline was Mrs. Hall's property. Missouri allowed slavery. In Alton, she would be free because Illinois was a free state.

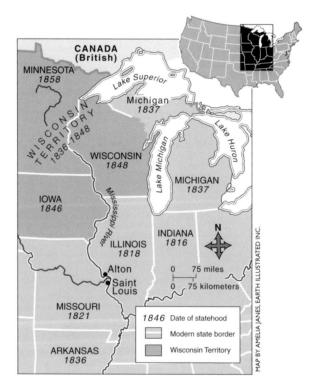

Although St. Louis, Missouri, and Alton, Illinois, are on opposite sides of the Mississippi River, Caroline would be closer to freedom in Alton.

3

Passing on the Mississippi

Crowds of
passengers waited
for the steamboat.
Caroline held on
tightly to her box
and the ticket. Then,
she saw a group of
girls about her age.

This steamboat schedule shows it would have taken
Caroline 2 hours to get to Alton from St. Louis.

Caroline had an
idea. If she could stay close to those girls, people might
think she was with their group. The girls were dressed nicely.
Caroline's green silk dress was probably a hand-me-down
from one of the women in the Hall family, but it was pretty.
Caroline slipped the silver necklace from her stepfather
around her neck and stepped closer to the girls.

The girls were also traveling across the Mississippi River to Alton. They stayed on deck in the sunshine. After the ship steamed away from the St. Louis shore, they probably noticed a dark-haired girl wearing a green dress. Maybe they smiled. Maybe she smiled back. Soon, they were sitting on deck, laughing and talking. The dark-haired girl sat down, too.

This silk dress from about 1840 is similar to the one that Caroline wore during her escape.

The July sun was still warm. The girls must have enjoyed the steamboat ride because soon they began to sing. Maybe they sang dancing songs such as "Cissy in the Barn," "Bow Belinda," or "Sally Down the Alley" because soon toes started tapping. Then, the girls began to dance. Even the dark-haired girl wearing the pretty, silver necklace joined in. They sang and danced as the steamboat headed toward Alton.

Imagine what Caroline felt as the steamship pulled away from St. Louis. She had left her grandmother and stepfather behind. She was leaving everything and everyone she knew and loved. But she was also leaving slavery behind.

The deck of Caroline's steamboat would have resembled this one from 1860.

And ahead was freedom. She probably experienced a strange mix of emotions—excitement, fear, sadness.

Caroline must have listened to the girls talking. They were students at the Monticello **Ladies' Seminary**, a school for rich, white girls. What did Caroline think as she edged closer to the group of girls? Would they think she was a white girl traveling alone? Would the other passengers think she was one of the schoolgirls?

ladies' seminary (se meh ner ee): a school where girls were taught to be proper ladies

11

Caroline crossed the river with the girls. When they sang, she sang. When they danced, so did she. She had to fit in. She had to convince everyone on the boat that she was just another white girl.

Monticello Ladies' Seminary, 1840

Today, we know the schoolgirls and passengers believed Caroline was white. We know she reached Alton, Illinois, safely. But at that time, Caroline didn't know what would happen. Every minute she must have worried. She must have looked at every person, wondering if they believed she was white. Or, would they recognize her as a runaway slave and call the police?

When the steamboat reached Alton, Caroline got off and began to walk away. No one called the police. No one chased her. So far, she was safe in a free state!

Caroline didn't know a single person in Alton. No friends met her at the steamboat dock. No family smiled and waved. As she walked away from the ship, a black man working on the docks saw that she was alone. He knew she needed help.

The man spoke to her. She might have fooled the schoolgirls and the passengers, but this man wasn't fooled. He asked if Caroline was an escaping slave. "No!" Caroline insisted. But this man didn't believe her.

Elijah Lovejoy

Alton, Illinois, wasn't a safe place for Caroline. Just 5 years earlier, an abolitionist had died for freedom in that city. Elijah Lovejoy published the *Alton Observer*, an antislavery newspaper. He was also a **preacher** who spoke and wrote against slavery whenever he could.

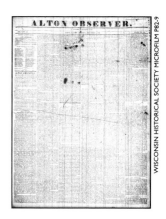

Reverend Lovejoy's antislavery newspaper the *Alton Observer*

preacher (preech ur): a person who gives a religious talk to people, especially during a church service

But proslavery people wanted to stop Lovejoy. They broke into his office and destroyed his printing press. He bought another. They destroyed it, too. Finally, a crowd of proslavery people set fire to Lovejoy's warehouse—with Lovejoy, his friends, and his printing press inside!

Abolitionist Elijah Lovejoy's printing press

Lovejoy ran outside to stop the men. Angry shouts and gunshots filled the air. He staggered back into the warehouse. "I've been shot!" he shouted. In minutes, Lovejoy was dead.

Lithograph by Henry Tanner depicting the angry mob burning Elijah Lovejoy's office on November 7, 1837

14

The black man who stopped Caroline on the dock knew that if proslavery people in Alton realized she was escaping, they would catch her and return her to her owners. Slave hunters and **bounty hunters** hung around Alton and other towns along the Mississippi River where **fugitive** slaves might come.

Plaque celebrating the life of Elijah Lovejoy

The black man told her she wasn't safe. He said she must get away from Alton. The next morning, he put her on a stagecoach headed north—far north. Her money had bought a ticket all the way to Milwaukee, Wisconsin.

bounty hunter (boun tee huhnt ur): a person who caught runaway slaves for money
fugitive (fyoo juh tiv): someone who is running away, especially from the police

4

Coming to Milwaukee

In 1842, cars hadn't been invented. Railroads had not yet crisscrossed the country, so trains traveled only between large cities. Most people made journeys in buggies, wagons, and stagecoaches pulled by horses. With a driver seated in front and the people crowded in back, coaches bumped along dusty roads or followed one-lane "highways." At night, they stopped at stagecoach inns to eat and sleep. Some inns were log cabins where coach passengers slept on the floor, rolled in blankets. Some inns looked more like houses, with beds and bedrooms.

Stagecoach pulled by horses

At the Milton House, a stagecoach inn in Milton, Wisconsin, people paid 25 cents for supper and 25 cents to sleep in fancy, "off the floor" beds. Customers paid 10 cents for food and water for their horses.

Milton House, a stagecoach inn

Caroline rode for long hours in the dusty, hot, crowded coach. Every day, she used more of her money to pay for meals cooked by the innkeepers when the coach stopped. Every day took her farther from home.

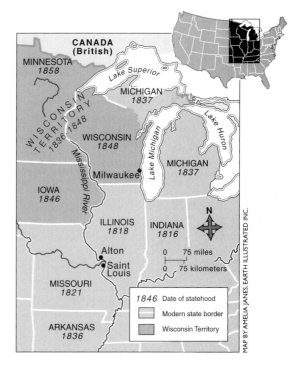

How long do you think the trip from Alton to Milwaukee took Caroline?

17

Caroline rode to the end of the line—Milwaukee, Wisconsin. When the coach finally rolled to a stop in front of the Milwaukee House Inn, Caroline got off. What a busy place! Horse-drawn buggies and wagons rolled by. People walked on wooden sidewalks. Horses were tied to hitching posts in front of wooden buildings. Just a few blocks away the blue water of Lake Michigan stretched to the horizon. Steamboats docked in the harbor.

WHI IMAGE ID 28046

Horse-drawn buggy in downtown Milwaukee, 1856

Caroline didn't know a single person. She was alone in a strange place. Her mind must have overflowed with questions and worries. Where would she stay? How would she take care of herself? Would she have enough money for food and a place to sleep until she could find a job?

Caroline wasn't alone for long. Very soon, it seemed, help arrived. A black man walked up and introduced himself. Robert Titball was his name. He smiled. He asked Caroline if she needed help. Titball was a barber. His shop was in the Milwaukee House Inn.

Not many black people lived in Milwaukee in 1842. Imagine how surprised and happy Caroline must have been to see a friendly face. To hear someone say, "Welcome. Do you need help?"

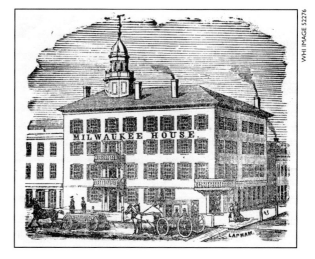

Milwaukee House Inn, 1857

The barber seemed kind. Caroline trusted him when he invited her to stay in his house. She trusted him when he offered to keep her money in a safe place. She trusted his friendship. And why shouldn't she? Titball was black. He had been a slave, too. He understood why Caroline had wanted freedom, even though it meant leaving behind everyone and everything she loved.

For a week or more, Caroline stayed in Titball's house. Perhaps she looked for a job. She wanted to make a home for herself in Milwaukee.

Meanwhile, back in St. Louis, Mr. and Mrs. Hall realized Caroline was gone. Of course, they were furious. Who would do Caroline's work now? Also, a strong woman like Caroline was worth at least $800, a great deal of money at that time.

Mr. Hall called the police. The police found out Caroline had escaped on a riverboat. In Missouri, black people weren't allowed to travel without papers proving they were free or a letter from the slave owner giving permission. The riverboat company had broken the law by selling a ticket to Caroline.

Mr. Hall **sued** the riverboat company for $800. If he couldn't have Caroline, at least he would have the money she was worth! In Missouri, anyone who helped a slave escape was punished. Of course, the riverboat owners didn't know Caroline was escaping when she bought the ticket. But the judge wouldn't care. He would still make them pay.

sued (**sood**): started a case against someone in a court of law

The riverboat company hired a lawyer, Matthew Spencer, to find Caroline. The company offered a $300 reward to whoever found Caroline. In 1842, a worker earned about $300 in a whole year. So $300 was a *huge* amount of money, but not as much as the riverboat company would have to pay to Mr. and Mrs. Hall if Caroline weren't found.

Matthew Spencer set out like a bloodhound, following Caroline's trail across the Mississippi River to Alton, and then to Wisconsin.

No one knows how Matthew Spencer discovered where Caroline had gone. It wasn't common for young women to travel alone then. Surely someone had noticed her. Somehow, Spencer discovered Caroline had traveled by coach to Wisconsin.

Back in Milwaukee, Caroline was still staying with the barber, Titball. She was probably happy to be free and starting a new life. But all that was about to end.

About a week after Caroline stepped off the stagecoach in front of the Milwaukee House Inn, Spencer and some men from St. Louis arrived in town. They were slave hunters, and Caroline was the prize they were hunting.

The very idea of slave hunters in their town made every Milwaukee abolitionist angry. Although Wisconsin was a free state, some people were against slavery, while other people didn't care about the issue. Most people had probably never even seen a slave.

Still, news spread about the $300 reward for Caroline. People who had never cared about slavery were suddenly interested. But they weren't worried about Caroline. They cared about getting rich.

News about slave hunters blew through Milwaukee like a storm. First, Spencer sent the slave hunters to look for Caroline. Then he went to find a lawyer in Milwaukee to get legal papers signed. Spencer planned to arrest Caroline— maybe for stealing the $100—and take her back to Missouri.

The slave hunters went to the neighborhood in Milwaukee where most black people lived. They asked everyone about Caroline. Maybe they offered money for information. Maybe they tried to frighten people. Soon, they found Titball. They wanted to know if he knew anything about a girl named Caroline.

The men were like wolves with prey in sight. Of course, the barber knew the men were slave hunters. He knew they would take Caroline back to slavery. But he also knew he might get some reward money. So Titball said Caroline was staying with him. He agreed to meet the slave hunters at his house. But secretly, he made another plan.

A neighborhood boy was nearby. Titball told him a story that must have made the boy's heart beat fast. Slave hunters were after the girl, Caroline, he said. Would the boy help her? Titball asked him to take Caroline from the house. He told the boy where to hide her so she'd be safe.

The boy had once been a slave running to freedom just like Caroline. He listened to Titball's story. But he didn't believe it. He just didn't trust the barber. He thought carefully. What should he do?

With every hour that passed, more people became involved in Caroline's story. Everyone had a different plan. Spencer and the slave hunters planned to catch her. Titball planned to keep her—until he got some of the reward money. And the boy had a plan of his own. He fetched Caroline. But the boy didn't do what Titball had told him to do. He took her to a secret place only *he* knew.

Soon, the freedom-loving people of the Underground Railroad would hear about Caroline and more plans would be made. In fact, a giant game of hide-and-seek would begin. The winner of this game would decide whether Caroline would spend the rest of her life as a slave or as a free person.

Underground Railroad sites in Wisconsin and Illinois

5

Crouching in a Barrel

Matthew Spencer said the law was on *his* side. After all, Caroline had stolen valuable property—herself. It's possible she also took money from Mr. Hall. It would be simple to get a few legal papers, arrest Caroline, and drag her back to slavery.

But abolitionists said the law was on *Caroline's* side. Slavery wasn't allowed in Wisconsin. Caroline might be valuable property in Missouri, but in Wisconsin, she was a free person.

Spencer called the abolitionists "Milwaukee **fanatics**." He knew he couldn't just grab Caroline and run, because the abolitionists would stop him. So, he decided to get around the "fanatics" by hiring a Milwaukee lawyer to get the legal papers to arrest her. Spencer probably expected to get

fanatic (fuh **nat** ik): a person who is very excited about a belief, cause, or interest

Caroline in a few days. How hard could it be for lawyers and expert slave hunters to capture one 16-year-old girl?

So, Spencer found a lawyer's office. Spencer told the lawyer all about Caroline, Titball, and the slave hunters. The lawyer was angry. He wanted nothing to do with slave catching. He told Spencer to leave and never come back.

The lawyer told people that he'd thrown Spencer right out of his office. He told the whole story about Caroline, Titball, and the slave hunters. Lots of people heard. Some thought it was a funny story. Some were horrified.

One man, Asahel Finch, realized that unless someone helped the runaway girl, the slave hunters would get her. Someone must stop them before it was too late.

Finch raced to the swampy neighborhood near the Milwaukee River where Milwaukee's black citizens lived. He searched everywhere for Caroline. He *had* to find the girl before Spencer and the slave hunters arrived.

No one knows how Finch found Caroline. Maybe he knocked on doors, begging people for help. Maybe he found the boy who'd figured out Titball's terrible plan and hid Caroline.

Somehow, Finch found the frightened girl in her hiding place. He had to tell Caroline that Titball had **betrayed** her.

How did Finch convince her to run away with him? After all, Robert Titball was black. Asahel Finch was white. Caroline thought Titball was her friend. No one knows what Finch said, because he never told. But somehow, Caroline did believe him.

By afternoon, Finch and Caroline were on the run. They hid near the river, crouching behind bushes and branches. They waited until night, when darkness would cover them and Caroline could escape.

betrayed (bee **trayd**): turned against someone, especially in a time of need

While Asahel Finch was frantically searching for Caroline, Spencer was busy, too. He found a lawyer named Jonathan Arnold who agreed to get the legal papers for Caroline's arrest.

Spencer returned to the slave hunters. All the legal papers were ready. The men must have been smiling as they headed toward Titball's house. They expected that by evening they would have the girl and be $300 richer.

Titball met Spencer and the slave hunters. He planned to demand part of the reward before he took them to Caroline.

Titball took the slave hunters to his house. Of course, Caroline wasn't there. The slave hunters panicked. They'd traveled hundreds of miles and spent more than a week chasing the girl. They couldn't lose her now.

Titball had tricked them. Spencer wasn't happy about it, but he agreed to give the barber $100. That was exactly what Titball wanted! He took them to the place where he'd told the boy to hide Caroline.

The men followed Titball down the streets and alleys along the river until they reached the hiding place. Now, it was the barber's turn to be tricked. Caroline wasn't there!

The slave hunters were furious. They grabbed Titball. Yelling and threatening, pushing and shoving, they threw him on the ground. Feet lifted to kick. Voices shouted.

Titball would get a terrific beating unless he could fool the men again. He begged. He lied. He claimed he wasn't trying to trick them. He was trying to help.

Titball must have been a talented liar, because Spencer and the other men let him go. He'd saved himself a beating, but he didn't get a penny of the reward money.

It was one of those long, warm August days when the sun is in no hurry to set. Asahel Finch and Caroline huddled in their hiding place near the river, waiting for darkness.

If they could get out of town, Finch could take her to an abolitionist's home where she'd be safe for one night at least.

As soon as the sky began to turn gray, Finch and Caroline crossed the river. They were afraid. What if the slave hunters were prowling the streets? What if they were seen in the moonlight? Finally, Finch decided the trip out of town was too risky. He would hide Caroline somewhere.

But where could she hide? They searched near the muddy riverbanks. The houses in that poor neighborhood looked like sheds, with a door in the front and, if the

Caroline and Asahel Finch searched along the banks of the Milwaukee River for a place to hide.

owners could afford it, a window or 2. The homes were built off the ground in case the river flooded.

Near the corner of Grand Avenue and Kilbourn Town, Finch and Caroline stopped. There, between the sidewalk and the road, they saw a barrel surrounded by weeds and grass.

This kind of barrel was known as a **hogshead** and was designed to keep sugar safe from mice and moisture. Could it also be used to keep Caroline safe from Spencer and his men?

WHI IMAGE ID 52872

Hogshead barrels

hogshead (**hogz** hed): type of wood or heavy pottery barrel that holds about 60 gallons

The barrel was in front of a house so small that folks passing by could stand on the sidewalk and see from the front door to the back window. On that hot August day, the front door was open. The owner of the tiny house was a black man.

Finch had to leave Caroline and find help. But could they trust the man in the little house? Once, Caroline might have thought she'd be safe among her own people. But Titball had betrayed her, and he was black. Yet now, Finch and Caroline had no choice. They had to trust someone. Caroline squeezed herself into the barrel, and Finch fastened the lid tightly and ran out of the neighborhood. He promised to come back in the morning with help. Unless, of course, Spencer and his men found Caroline first.

6

A Ticket on the Underground Railroad

History isn't like math. In math, if you have 2 baskets and put 2 apples in each one, the number of apples will always be equal. But, in history, 2 memories of the same event aren't always the same. Caroline's story is like that.

Some people said Caroline stayed in the sugar barrel for an entire night. Some said she was there, cramped and hot, all night *and* the next day. Lyman Goodnow, an abolitionist who helped Caroline get to Canada, said she was picked up late that night. Another abolitionist named Chauncey Olin wrote that she stayed in the barrel for 2 or 3 whole days!

Historians know that Caroline did hide in the barrel. Asahel Finch did return with a wagon. It was probably under cover of darkness—late that night or before daylight the following day. With Caroline hidden under hay in the back, he drove the wagon outside the city to a farmhouse owned by his friend, Samuel Brown.

Freedom-loving people knew and respected Samuel Brown. He was a good man who strongly stood against slavery. And, most important, Brown knew every abolitionist in the whole area. He knew who could be trusted and who couldn't.

So, whether Caroline arrived in the middle of the night or just in time for breakfast, she did find a safe hiding place with Samuel Brown. And, although she didn't know it, she was about to start another part of her journey on the Underground Railroad.

It was a good thing Brown didn't actually have to buy a ticket on this freedom railroad, because he was very poor. His house was small and his wagon was so **rickety** that it was falling apart. But he welcomed Caroline into his tiny home as an honored guest. And the next morning he hitched his horse to the creaky, old wagon, threw a saddle in the back, and headed off to Prairieville—now called Waukesha—to take Caroline to friends on the Underground Railroad.

rickety (**rik** uh tee): old, weak, and likely to break

Samuel Brown was worried. He knew his wagon would fall apart if he tried to drive fast. The roads between Milwaukee and Prairieville were just muddy wheel tracks. Rocks and holes could break wagon wheels. But they had to take these roads to reach his friends.

Caroline's first stop on the Underground Railroad was Prairieville (now named Waukesha).

As the wagon rattled along toward the main road, Samuel Brown heard men's voices. He pulled over and stopped. Then he saw the men. Oh no! It was Spencer, the slave hunters, and the lawyer Jonathan Arnold riding straight toward them.

Roads at the time were rutted and difficult to travel on.

36

The men rode by, just a few feet from the wagon. Where was Caroline? Maybe she huddled under the hay in the back of the wagon. Maybe she was sitting next to Samuel Brown, wrapped in a shawl or wearing a bonnet to hide her face. No one knows. But the men were so close that Caroline could hear them talk and, maybe, even watch them ride by. Caroline and Samuel Brown were probably terrified! And who wouldn't be?

Once the slave hunters had passed, Brown drove as fast as he dared. But the rickety wagon broke down. There was no time to waste. The slave hunters could return.

Brown unhitched his horse and dragged the saddle from the back of the wagon. They both climbed on the horse's back and rode toward the tiny farm town of Lisbon. There Samuel and Lucinda **Daugherty** lived. The Daughertys could be counted on for help. They stood solidly against slavery. There, Caroline would be safe. At least, that's what Brown hoped.

Daugherty (doe er tee)

While Caroline hid with the Daugherty family, the slave hunters, Spencer, and Jonathan Arnold started a game of hide-and-seek. They rented rooms at the Prairieville House, a tavern and hotel. From there, they rode all over the countryside. These slave catchers knocked on doors; searched houses, barns, and fields; and offered rewards for Caroline's capture.

WHI IMAGE ID 52836

"Samuel Brown…took her to my father's house near Pewaukee, all of 20 miles, not daring to go in the roadway any of the way, so hot were the **pursuers** on her track."
—Almira Daugherty Woodruff, *The History of Waukesha County*, 1880

Word continued to spread about Caroline. When people realized they could earn $300 just for catching a girl, they joined the hide-and-seek game, too. Caroline and her new friends on the Underground Railroad were in real danger. Neighbors spied on neighbors. Friends suddenly couldn't be trusted. Nice people became slave hunters.

pursuer (per **soo** er): a person chasing someone in order to catch him or her

WHI IMAGE ID 12176

View of Prairieville (Waukesha), 1857

While everyone seemed to be talking about Caroline, abolitionists pretended they weren't interested. They did their best to act as though they didn't know anything. The reward money drew people like a magnet. People watched day and night on all the bridges and roads.

Spencer and his friends kept searching and asking questions. Once, a large group of slave hunters in Prairieville crouched all night in the bushes outside an abolitionist's

39

house just because someone had hinted that Caroline might be inside. Abolitionists were followed, spied on, and threatened by total strangers. The lawyers, Matthew Spencer and Jonathan Arnold, kept saying the law was on their side. They said anyone who helped Caroline might be arrested, too.

One abolitionist was Ezra Mendall. As a young man, he'd been famous for getting into fights. But by the time Caroline arrived in Prairieville, he was a deacon, or a leader, in the First Congregational Church. He was more than 60 years old but still strong and not afraid of anyone. He wasn't afraid to fight slave hunters.

One day, the slave hunters found Ezra Mendall working in his potato field. Jonathan Arnold waved a **warrant** in front of the old man. Arnold screamed, "You are **harboring** that slave-girl, which is against the law."

"Well, a bad law is sometimes better broken than obeyed," said Mendall.

warrant (wor uhnt): a legal paper that gives permission for something, like to search property or to arrest a person
harboring (har bur ing): hiding someone

When Mendall glanced at his rifle nearby, Arnold stopped yelling. He demanded to search Mendall's house.

"No, sir, you don't search my house for any slave," said Mendall. The crowd, afraid of the rifle, marched back to Prairieville. A man more than 60 years of age had single-handedly frightened away the whole **posse**. And what a posse! The men were armed with pistols, whiskey, and arrest warrants!

While Mendall was scaring away the slave hunters, Caroline was safely hidden at the Daughertys' house. At least, everyone hoped she was safe. No one whispered a word about her hiding place.

Edward Matthews visited the Daughertys while Caroline was there. Matthews was a traveling preacher who liked to say, "I preached for God and against slavery" everywhere he went. He'd been yelled at and beaten for speaking against slavery. He'd been thrown out of churches, halls, and whole towns by proslavery mobs.

posse (**poss** ee): a group of people gathered together to help catch a criminal

One Friday afternoon, Pastor Matthews sat at the kitchen table with the Daugherty family and Caroline. They were enjoying a cup of tea when, suddenly, the door opened. A neighbor walked right into the house without knocking or even saying *hello*.

There sat Caroline. The neighbor took one look at her, turned around, and walked back out the door.

For a moment, everyone was silent with shock. The neighbor was no friend to slaves. Maybe he would turn Caroline over to Spencer. Maybe not. But everyone knew one thing for certain: Caroline was in danger.

Now that Caroline's hiding place was no longer a secret, the game of hide-and-seek was about to become even wilder and more terrifying.

7

Up the Potato Chute

The action in Prairieville was heating up. Greedy for reward money, the Daughertys' neighbor did just as they had feared. He headed straight to Spencer and the slave hunters. He'd seen the girl!

It was just what the slave hunters had been waiting for! They didn't waste time. They set out for the Daughertys' house the very next day.

The Daughertys' farm sat in the middle of a large, open prairie. From the farmhouse window, they could see any traveler on the Prairieville Road from a mile away.

That afternoon, Caroline sat at the window. Several men on horseback appeared on the road. She watched as they passed by the first side road and then the second. They kept coming, straight toward the Daughertys' house. Those men were after her!

Samuel Daugherty was gone. As quickly as possible, Lucinda Daugherty, her daughter Anne, and Caroline made a plan. Of course, Caroline couldn't stay in the house. But, if Spencer and the slave hunters were close enough that Caroline could see them on the road, they were close enough to see her escape. Also, the house was small, with only a front door. How could she escape?

As the men reached the door, Caroline rushed to the cellar. Down in the cellar, Anne boosted Caroline on top of a barrel. Then, she helped Caroline scramble into the potato **chute**, a wall opening used to roll potatoes from outside the house into barrels in the cellar.

Caroline pulled and scratched her way up the potato chute. Then she crawled on her hands and knees until she reached the end of the field. She crouched behind the cornstalks to hide.

chute (**shoot**): a narrow, tilted passage for goods, garbage, laundry, grain, or coal

Lucinda Daugherty knew that every second she kept the men in the house gave Caroline another second to escape. Imagine how her mind must have whirled, trying to think of ways to distract the slave hunters while Caroline crept away.

The men reached the steps and banged on the door. Lucinda grabbed a bucket of water and began to scrub the floor. She probably acted as if the men had interrupted her housework. And even bold slave hunters might wait a moment before walking on a wet, newly washed floor.

The men demanded to know where Caroline was hiding. Lucinda wasn't afraid of them. She told them exactly what she thought of them. She said no honest, good person would chase a 16-year-old girl. She wondered if the slave hunters didn't know the difference between right and wrong.

The men demanded to search the house. Not only did Lucinda Daugherty let them search, she helped them! She told the men to open every door and look in every room and hallway. The slave hunters must have been astonished as the woman led them over every inch of the farmhouse. Did they climb to the bedrooms upstairs? Stoop down and peer under the beds? Did they poke into closets and drawers? Of course they climbed down into the cellar. But in the cool cellar where Caroline had been just a few minutes before, they found only barrels of food.

Lucinda Daugherty had succeeded. She had gained time for Caroline to escape. The slave hunters searched the barn and questioned the hired man, but he didn't know a thing and hadn't seen a thing. The men must have searched the cornfield, too. But they didn't find Caroline.

Finally, the slave hunters gave up. They knew the girl had been seen at the Daughertys' house the day before. But she now was nowhere to be found.

Still, the game of hide-and-seek continued. The summer days were long, with sunlight until 8:00 or 9:00 at night, so the slave hunters had time to head back to Prairieville. Meanwhile, Samuel Daugherty came home and heard the

Illustration of slave catchers pointing guns at runaway slaves—just what Caroline was trying to avoid!

terrifying story. Only luck and quick thinking had kept Caroline from being captured. Samuel knew they couldn't wait even one more day. Caroline had to leave. Only the abolitionists in Prairieville could help her.

So, Samuel Daugherty raced to Prairieville. The slave hunters were still there. Soon, even Caroline herself would be in Prairieville.

The slave hunters weren't happy. They'd expected it would be easy to find and catch Caroline. But nothing was easy about it. They'd wasted a whole afternoon chasing her. Lucinda Daugherty had made them look like fools. And they

weren't an inch closer to finding the girl than they'd been
2 days earlier.

On the way from the Daugherty house back to Prairieville,
the slave hunters had **spied** an abolitionist, Mr. Wheelock,
working in his field. Wheelock was known for telling the
truth, so the men decided to find out what he knew about
Caroline.

The slave hunters quickly thought up a plan and a lie.
"We need your help," they told Wheelock. They said Caroline
missed her family and wanted to go home. "Help us find the
girl," the slave hunters said, "and we'll take her safely back to
St. Louis."

The slave hunters painted a touching picture of a poor,
homesick girl who missed her family. But Wheelock didn't
believe it.

Then, the slave hunters told an even more outrageous
lie. They said if Caroline didn't want to return to St. Louis,
Spencer would give her "free papers" and let her go.

spied (spyed): sighted

"Do you know where she is?" they asked Wheelock.

He only replied, "No." Then, it was Wheelock's turn to do some quick thinking. Wheelock said if Caroline really did want to go home, he would gladly find her.

Wheelock said he couldn't make such a big decision alone. He'd have to talk with another abolitionist, Edmund Clinton. If Clinton agreed, Wheelock would bring him to meet the slave hunters at the Prairieville House at 10:00 that night.

The slave hunters were thrilled. Their lie had worked! They thought because Wheelock was extremely honest that he was also extremely stupid. They were wrong.

Wheelock acted as if he was completely fooled by the slave hunters' lies. But actually, he didn't believe a single word they said.

Wheelock raced to Clinton's house. They had to keep the slave hunters away from Caroline. They sent a boy to fetch Ezra Mendall, the rifle-**toting** old man.

toting (**toht** ing): carrying or hauling something

When Mendall arrived, plans quickly came together. Wheelock and Clinton would keep the slave hunters busy at the Prairieville House. Mendall would get Caroline. He would stay off the roads and take Caroline away as far and fast as possible.

When the clocks chimed 10:00, Wheelock and Clinton strolled into the Prairieville House. They each pulled up a chair and began to talk with Spencer and the other slave hunters.

The slave hunters believed their lie had worked. Wheelock and Clinton let them believe it. They stayed until midnight, drinking whiskey and talking. Then, Wheelock and Clinton stood up. "We won't have anything to do with you or your slave hunting," they announced. They turned and walked out the door!

While his friends were keeping the slave hunters busy, Mendall was sneaking Caroline into town. She hid with Clinton's own brother! The game of hide-and-seek was becoming more and more risky.

The next morning was Sunday. The slave hunters were still angry and empty-handed. They didn't know Caroline was only blocks away, eating breakfast with Mrs. Clinton. The rest of the Clinton family walked into church along with Lyman Goodnow, Wheelock, Mendall, and nearly every abolitionist in Prairieville.

Goodnow, a **bachelor** farmer and Clinton's brother-in-law, was about to play a part in the game of hide-and-seek. And this game would take all that night—and many more nights after that.

Here's what Goodnow himself had to say about what happened:

> [A] man came to me after church, and told me to have my team ready that night…a mile west of the village in oak openings, prepared for anything.…
> I knew what that meant.
>
> I did not dare to take my own horses out, for I was watched; but I told him I would be at the place with

bachelor (**bach** uh lur): an unmarried man

51

horses. So I went to [an abolitionist friend] and said, "I want your horses to-night and I don't want you should ask me a question." [My friend] let me have his team, a splendid one, of which he thought everything.

I took the horses after dark, and went to the woods.... After awhile I heard a whistle and answered it. **By-and-by** ...Allen Clinton...made his appearance on horseback with Caroline riding with him....Caroline was given into my hands. I chose Mendall as company and we started with Caroline curled down in the straw at the bottom of the wagon...[headed] for—we had no idea where, but to any place of safety.

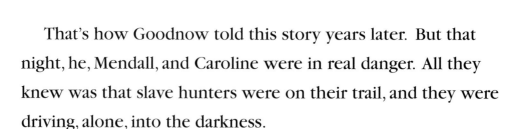

That's how Goodnow told this story years later. But that night, he, Mendall, and Caroline were in real danger. All they knew was that slave hunters were on their trail, and they were driving, alone, into the darkness.

by-and-by (**bye** and **bye**): later, after some time has passed

8

Getaway!

With Caroline huddled under the hay in the wagon bed, Goodnow and Mendall drove all night. They traveled more than 30 miles. Near midnight, they passed through Mukwonago and headed toward Spring Prairie. In Spring Prairie, they knew abolitionists who would help them. Hour after hour they drove,

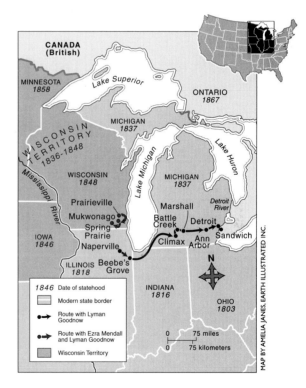

The last leg of Caroline's journey to freedom

keeping away from the main roads. They used darkness and shadows to hide. The wagon rattled across prairie land and shallow creek beds. The 2 men listened for every sound. The slave hunters might be chasing them.

As the sun rose, they headed to the Thompson farm in Spring Prairie. Charles Thompson was a trusted, antislavery man. They could count on him for help.

But as they reached the farm, Goodnow and Mendall didn't stop. They didn't even slow down. Thompson's fields were filled with workers harvesting crops. There were too many people who might spot Caroline.

The exhausted men kept driving. They'd just have to find help from someone else.

About an hour later, Goodnow and Mendall guided the team and wagon across Honey Creek. They stopped in front of a small log house on the open prairie. Mendall climbed down from the wagon and knocked on the cabin door.

Solomon Dwinnell answered the door. He must have been shocked to find Ezra Mendall standing in the doorway so early in the morning. With him was a girl—Caroline.

Mendall said, "We have work for you. The girl is hotly **pursued**, and a large reward is offered, and many are out hunting for her. We ask you to [hide] her today, and to-night remove her to another place so she cannot be captured. We will come in a few days and take her."

Dwinnell was a strong abolitionist. He would do whatever he could to help Caroline. But, as Goodnow and Mendall turned to leave, Solomon Dwinnell noticed the look on Caroline's face.

She was terrified. She stared at the white stranger. She looked anxiously at Goodnow and Mendall. Finally, she cried out, "Are you leaving me with friends? Am I safe here?"

Imagine being in Caroline's place. She didn't know whom to trust. She'd been betrayed, chased, and threatened. Now, she was being left with strangers again.

Goodnow and Mendall promised Caroline that she would be safe. But they couldn't stay. She had no choice except to trust their promise.

pursued (per **sood**): chased or followed by someone

The slave hunters might figure out where the 3 had gone and come looking for them, so Goodnow and Mendall left Caroline and started for home. But as the tired horses plodded north toward Prairieville, Goodnow discovered a surprise hidden in the straw beneath his seat.

On the way home, moving my feet around in the straw, I hit something hard;...picking it up it proved to be the longest butcher-knife I ever saw. I said, "Deacon, what's this?" "Oh, it's something I brought along to pick my teeth with," said the deacon.

You can guess what he intended to do if anyone [tried] to capture us. I was glad enough no one [tried]...for if we had been attacked, there would have been some dead slave hunters as sure as life.

Goodnow and Mendall returned to Prairieville. They slipped into town without a word to anyone. No one had noticed they were gone. What relief! For that day, at least, Caroline was safe.

9

Eight Dollars and a Borrowed Saddle: A Journey to See the Queen

Goodnow and Mendall felt the worry slide from their shoulders. They'd tricked Spencer and the rest of the slave hunters. But just as quickly as the worry left, it returned.

The abolitionists in Prairieville knew and trusted Solomon Dwinnell. But, the more they talked and thought, the more afraid they became. They remembered how Caroline had been found at the Daughertys' in spite of their careful planning. Was Dwinnell a careful planner? Had news of Caroline and the reward money reached as far away as Spring Prairie? Finally, the men decided Caroline wasn't safe anywhere in Wisconsin. She must go to Canada.

The abolitionists talked late into the night. They searched for a plan to get Caroline safely away. Caroline couldn't go alone. Someone had to take her. But who? And how?

Mendall was too old for such a long, hard trip. The Clinton brothers had wives and little children. Nobody had any extra money.

It would take at least 5 weeks in a horse-drawn wagon to reach Canada and return. Who could just pick up and leave for more than a month? It was August, and everyone had crops to harvest.

Although no one said it aloud, everyone knew the trip could be dangerous. If slave hunters found Caroline, they would take her. They might hurt or even kill anyone who helped her.

Finally, everyone looked at Lyman Goodnow. He was a bachelor without a wife or children who needed him. He was strong and willing. And everyone knew he was fiercely against slavery. Goodnow agreed. He would take Caroline to Canada.

Once the decision was made, the abolitionists didn't waste any time. They'd have to find a horse, a small wagon or buggy, and some money. Of course, they must not be seen. Spencer and the slave hunters were still staying at the Prairieville House and searching the countryside.

The game of hide-and-seek had to end. Either Caroline would be found and returned to slavery or she would reach Canada and freedom. Everything depended on Goodnow, his friends in Prairieville, and Caroline's courage.

It was nearly night. As the sky grew dark, Goodnow led his horse to Edmund Clinton's blacksmith shop. The horse wasn't saddled. Anyone watching would think it just needed new shoes. No one would imagine Goodnow was planning a trip.

Edmund Clinton waited in the dim light. He knew Goodnow hadn't come for horseshoes. He'd come for help. Goodnow asked for a big favor—a saddle, a bridle, and all the money Clinton had. Then he said, "I am going on a skeerup, and I may...pay the Queen a visit before I get back."

A "skeerup" was a quick, risky trip. The joke about the queen meant he was headed for Canada, a country ruled by England's Queen Victoria.

Clinton fetched his own saddle and bridle. He emptied his wallet. Five dollars was all the cash he had. Goodnow had $3. Goodnow set off for a 500-mile trip with $8, a farm horse, and a borrowed saddle and bridle!

Quietly, the men saddled the horse. With a quick good-bye and a handshake, Goodnow started for Spring Prairie. The sky was moonless and black as ink. The good news was no slave hunter would see him. The bad news was Goodnow couldn't see either! By midnight, he was lost. A cold rain began to fall. By 7:00 in the morning, he was soaked to the skin and shivering. It was noon when he finally arrived, hungry and falling-down tired, at Dwinnell's house. Caroline was gone. So was Dwinnell.

For a moment, Goodnow panicked. Where was Caroline? Had slave hunters found her?

Goodnow hurried to the next town. Maybe Caroline was hiding with abolitionists there. Sure enough, he found her at Peffer's farm in Gardner's Prairie. News had spread about the plan to help Caroline escape, and soon 3 or 4 other abolitionists arrived at Peffer's house.

One of the abolitionists was Dr. Edward Dyer. He was known as far away as Chicago as a leader in the fight against slavery. In his hometown of Burlington, Wisconsin, he'd named the street in front of his house "Liberty Avenue." No one who saw that name questioned his ideas about slavery and freedom!

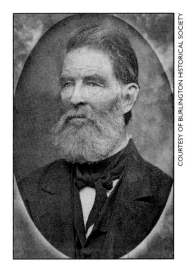

Dr. Edward Dyer

Edward Dyer took charge. Obviously, Goodnow couldn't take Caroline to Canada on horseback. They needed help. One abolitionist offered his horse and buggy. Dyer brought a pillowcase filled with food. Right there, standing in front of Peffer's farmhouse, Dyer took up a collection. He asked the men to give as much as they could. In addition to Goodnow's $8, they collected a total of $20.

Finally, Dr. Dyer wrote a letter begging all freedom-loving people between Wisconsin and Canada to help Caroline and Goodnow. At that time, doctors were well respected in the community, so a letter from a doctor would carry a lot of weight with most people. Afterward, people said the letter "would almost stir the heart of a stone."

The gifts encouraged Goodnow and Caroline. For a moment, the wild plan to go to Canada seemed a little less impossible. Then Goodnow saw 2 men on horseback riding slowly up the hill. No! His heart beat faster. The men were Spencer and Arnold! The slave-hunting lawyers were still searching for Caroline. And there she was, with Goodnow and the abolitionists, standing in plain sight in the yard.

Monument to Dr. Edward Dyer in Burlington, Wisconsin

What could they do? If they ran to hide, they might just attract more attention. If they stayed in the yard, they might be seen. They waited. Every second must have seemed like an hour as Spencer and Arnold rode by. When the men disappeared over the top of the hill, relief must have flooded over everyone. It was only luck that Caroline and Goodnow hadn't been seen.

The abolitionists hid Goodnow and Caroline until night. Their plan was to head south, into Illinois. They would get help from abolitionist friends along the way. They'd hide during the day and travel at night.

Caroline hid in the floor of a buggy similar to this one.

Caroline curled up on the buggy floor, covered by a buffalo fur. The buggy bumped and bounced until she was bruised and sore. Yet they drove on, mile after mile after mile.

63

The plan worked. One abolitionist sent them to another. Mile by mile, day by day, they traveled around Chicago toward Indiana. Each day was a frightening adventure.

WHI IMAGE ID 47097

A veil, like the one worn here, meant Caroline could ride beside Goodnow.

In the countryside west of Chicago, they stayed in the little town of Naperville. Young ladies from the church noticed Caroline's ripped dress, stained with dirt and sweat. They brought her clean clothes and a cloth bag to hold her precious jewelry. That jewelry and her memories were all she had of her family and home.

Someone in Naperville had an excellent idea. Riding on the buggy floor was a torture for Caroline. So, the young ladies brought gloves and a dark-colored veil for her to wear. In 1842, women often used veils to keep dust and sun from their faces. No one would think it strange to see a lady with a veil. At last, Caroline could sit beside Goodnow on the buggy seat, and they could travel during the day.

10

Aboard the Underground Railroad

Caroline and Goodnow left Naperville. As they drove, Caroline told Goodnow about her life in St. Louis. She told him that Mrs. Hall had cut her hair and how she'd decided to run away. She told how she felt and what she was thinking. She might have whispered that she was sad and lonely. Or, she might have wondered out loud whether she had made a mistake in leaving her family and friends.

As the days passed, Caroline and Goodnow became more than just a person who needed help and someone helping. They became friends.

Caroline was afraid. Goodnow also worried about slave hunters. When the 2 reached the little town of Beebe's Grove, southeast of Chicago, they were shocked to discover just how right they'd been to feel worried and afraid.

They'd been sent to the home of Mr. and Mrs. Beebe. Mr. Beebe had always spoken against slavery, but this was the first time he could do more than talk. He was thrilled to help Caroline. He welcomed her into his home.

In a few minutes, the tired travelers were seated in a bright, cheerful kitchen. Plates of hot food were set before them. As they rested and ate, Beebe told them about his trip to Chicago just a day or so earlier.

WHI IMAGE ID 52550

Chicago harbor, around 1840

Beebe traveled to the city for business. He enjoyed the people and noise. He liked to walk on the docks in Chicago harbor, watching the ships and beautiful Lake Michigan. On this trip, Beebe said, he'd seen a poster offering a reward for a runaway slave. The poster described a girl. Three hundred dollars reward was offered for her capture. Caroline and Goodnow were horrified. That poster was for Caroline! If Chicago slave hunters saw that poster, they could be chasing her, too.

What they didn't know was that the poster was put up by the steamboat company that had sold Caroline a ticket so long ago in St. Louis. The company had hired a man to put posters at the Alton, Chicago, Milwaukee, and Michigan ports and all points in between. Caroline was in even greater danger than they had thought!

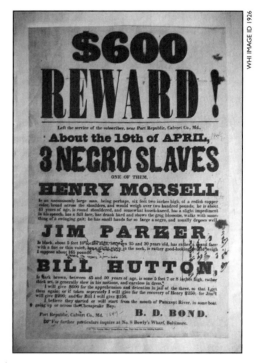

A reward poster like this one from 1849 was posted for the return of Caroline.

In spite of the upsetting news about the reward poster, Caroline and Goodnow agreed to go with the Beebes to a church meeting after dinner. The Beebes said every person in the church was an abolitionist. They had nothing to fear.

The church met at a little schoolhouse. Caroline and Goodnow sat in the front row. Mr. Beebe told everyone Caroline's story. People must have gasped as he told them about the slave hunters and the sugar barrel. When he explained how Caroline crawled up the potato chute and hid in the field at the Daughertys', they were probably shocked. In 1842, many people thought girls were weak and fragile. They couldn't imagine that a girl could crawl through fields and run from slave hunters.

After the meeting, the people strolled outside, enjoying the cool evening air. Everyone wanted to talk with Caroline. The church members were against slavery. Yet this was the first time that most of them had probably ever met anyone who had actually *been* a slave.

Caroline must have been exhausted. Still, she smiled and tried to politely answer questions. But she had a question of her own. In front of the church someone had built a wooden pole as tall as a pine tree. She'd never seen such a thing.

Some young women approached. "What is that?" Caroline asked.

They said it was a liberty pole.

"What is it for?" asked Caroline.

"For freedom," the young ladies said. "To [remember] the birth of liberty in America."

A 121-foot liberty pole was built in Stevens Point, Wisconsin, in 1869.

Maybe Caroline was bothered by the idea of people needing a pole to remind them of freedom. Maybe she just didn't understand. Caroline had not yet learned to read or write, but she was smart and quick thinking. She began to ask questions the young ladies couldn't answer.

"What do you do with it?" asked Caroline.

"Oh, look at it," they said.

"Who is allowed to look at it?"

"Why…everyone."

"You said it was a liberty pole. Can a slave look at it?"

The young women didn't know what to say. What would a liberty pole mean to a slave who didn't have freedom? Was the pole a way of showing that the little town of Beebe's Grove believed in freedom? Or did the people build the pole so they could feel good, thinking they had done something about liberty—even though millions of people were in slavery?

More about Liberty Poles

Since before the Revolutionary War, Americans have built wooden liberty poles in towns, in cities, and even in front of their houses. Some people hung flags or signs on the poles. It was a way of saying, "This is what I think, and I want everyone to know it."

In 1856, some Wisconsin people actually took the name Liberty Pole for their town. It was an election year. The country was divided—slave states against free states. James Buchanan was running for president, but he refused to take a stand against slavery. So, people in Ripon, Wisconsin, and elsewhere started a new political party. This was the birth of the Republican party. The Republicans chose a candidate who promised to end slavery, Senator John Frémont. John Frémont chose a liberty pole as the symbol for his **campaign** for president.

On September 10, folks in the tiny village of Bad Axe, Wisconsin, celebrated the new Republican party by building a 160-foot liberty pole in the center of town. About 500 people came to see the pole raised. Some traveled an entire day. People gave speeches against slavery and for John Frémont. Everyone cheered as the town voted to change its name. Today, you can still visit Liberty Pole, Wisconsin, near Viroqua.

campaign (kam **payn**): a series of actions organized to win something, such as a political election

Caroline and Goodnow left Beebe's Grove the next day with directions to the home of Quaker friends in Indiana. In the Quaker religion, peace was a guiding idea. Quakers also

Left to Right: Abolitionists Edward Harwood, Dr. William Brisbane, and Levi Coffin

worked hard against slavery. An Indiana Quaker named Levi Coffin was the so-called president of the Underground Railroad. He and his wife, Catherine, looked like gentle grandparents. In fact, they were fierce fighters against slavery. Over the years, in their house they hid more than 2,000 people running from slavery. They may have believed in peace, but they risked their lives, stared down slave hunters, and spent much of their money helping people get to freedom in Canada.

As Caroline and Goodnow left Beebe's Grove, the sky began to sprinkle rain. Soon, the wind began to howl. By late afternoon, the sky was black and rain poured down. There was no way they could reach the Quaker settlement and the next station on the Underground Railroad. They had to escape from the storm.

Finding a place to stay in a storm was the easy part. The hard part would be making sure no one saw Caroline's face. Even in Indiana, they couldn't trust any strangers. Anyone could be a **traitor**. Anyone could be a slave hunter.

The wind whipped. Rain soaked them to the skin. They came to a tiny, one-room cabin and pounded on the door. A young German husband and wife answered. "Please. Could we have shelter for the night?" Goodnow asked. The kind people invited them into the cabin.

How good the warm fire felt! Caroline and Goodnow shivered with cold.

Inside, they could barely see. The couple was so poor they couldn't even afford candles. The only light came from the fireplace. Caroline shared the corn husk mattress with the

traitor (**tray** tur): a person who is false to a friend, cause, or trust

73

wife. The husband and Goodnow wrapped themselves in blankets by the fire. They slept in the dark, woke in the dark, and munched cold corn bread and sipped water in the dark. Then, before sunrise, they thanked their kind hosts and left.

Later, Goodnow laughed as he told this story. In the dim firelight, the German couple never saw Caroline's face. The young wife never knew she'd shared her bed with a fugitive slave.

11

Safe and Not-So-Safe

For 3 days, Caroline and Goodnow traveled through Indiana, staying with Quaker families. All the Quaker men had gone to a church meeting. Only the women and children were home.

Each day, Caroline and Goodnow pushed themselves and their poor horse to travel another 20 or 30 miles. Each night, they were welcomed by a kind, Quaker woman at another station on the Underground Railroad. When they asked for food and a place to sleep, each woman answered in the soft, Quaker way, "**Thee** can have what thee wants." But none of the women would say a word about the Underground Railroad, in case Caroline and Goodnow might be traitors. Each woman sent them on to another Quaker family. Each day brought them closer to Michigan.

thee: an old word for you

75

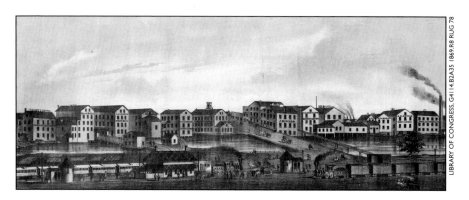

Battle Creek, Michigan, around 1869

On the fourth day, they left the Indiana Quaker settlement and crossed into Michigan. Their journey was almost over. In good weather, they'd need just 2 days to reach Battle Creek, then another 4 or 5 days to get to Detroit. Every day, they were closer to Canada. But every day they drove for hours on bumpy roads. The horse smelled. They smelled. Dust and sweat. Sweat and dust. They were sore and hot and just plain tired.

Southern Michigan was Underground Railroad territory. The people in Battle Creek and Ann Arbor were against slavery and were willing to help anyone escaping to freedom.

Caroline and Goodnow knew the names of abolitionists in Battle Creek, but that was too far to reach in a single day. By late afternoon, they were still 5 miles from the nearest town. Their poor horse couldn't go one more mile. They had to stop. On the prairie, outside the tiny village of Climax, they saw a farmhouse. They decided to take a risk and knocked on the door.

A gentleman answered. Of course, Caroline and Goodnow didn't tell the stranger who they really were. Perhaps they just said they were tired travelers who needed beds for the night. In those days, travelers could drive for an entire day without seeing a single town. So, it wasn't unusual for travelers to ask for a room or even a place to sleep on the floor of a farmhouse or cabin.

The man invited them in. At first, everything seemed fine. The man offered them food and then led Caroline to a small room with a cozy bed and an old-fashioned, wooden loom in the corner. After a long day bumping along in the buggy, that bed must have looked like heaven to Caroline. She slipped off her dress and hung it on the loom, along with the small, cloth bag that held the jewelry from her stepfather and some money Goodnow had given her. She climbed into bed and sank into a sleep as cozy as a warm blanket.

The next morning, Caroline and Goodnow woke early. To reach Battle Creek by night, they couldn't waste a minute. Perhaps they ate a quick breakfast. Perhaps the man offered them hot coffee and bread to eat on the way. But in the rush to leave, Caroline left the cloth bag that held the money and her precious jewelry hanging on the wooden loom.

Caroline left the bag with her jewelry and money on a loom, like the one shown here.

All day they drove. They squinted into the early-morning sun. They probably stopped to water and feed the horse at about noon. Then they pushed on toward Battle Creek.

About midafternoon, Caroline suddenly cried out: No! Stop! She realized she'd left behind her money and jewelry at the man's house in Climax. She couldn't go to Canada without them!

They were 20 miles from Climax—a whole day's drive. They could turn back, but that would mean driving 40 more miles. It would take 2 days! Their horse was weary. Caroline and Goodnow were weary. But the jewelry and money were important to Caroline. What should they do?

Finally, Goodnow decided to keep going to Battle Creek. He would stop in Climax on his trip home. It would be simple enough to collect the bag containing the jewelry and the money and send them to Caroline in Canada by mail. It must have broken Caroline's heart, but she agreed.

After a night with abolitionist friends in Battle Creek, Caroline and Goodnow followed the main road straight east, toward Detroit. Every mile brought Caroline closer to Canada and freedom.

The friends in Battle Creek sent them to Ann Arbor. They gave Caroline and Goodnow the name of Guy Beckley, editor of the local abolitionist newspaper, *Signal of Liberty*. His house was a station on the Underground Railroad. But before they reached the Beckleys' big, brick house in Ann Arbor, another adventure was waiting for them.

The day was pleasant and warm. The buggy rolled up gentle hills and past long, peaceful stretches of forest and farms. Caroline and Goodnow must have felt safe because they followed the main road, even in the daytime. It seems they weren't the only people who felt safe. Just outside the city of Marshall, Goodnow stopped the buggy in the middle of the road. There, in the open, he saw a gang of people—32 people escaping from slavery! Three men led them. They were armed, probably with axes or farm tools rather than guns. These were men ready to defend themselves and their friends.

Every day, while the group hid, the 3 leaders crept ahead, looking for Underground Railroad stations, food, and the safest routes to travel. Then, when the leaders thought it was safe, the whole group set out on foot. With them was an older woman. Goodnow thought she must have weighed 400 pounds. She could barely walk and had to be carried. Still, the group didn't leave her behind. The young men supported and carried the old woman. Day by day, mile by mile, 32 courageous people were making their way to Canada to be free.

That night, or perhaps the next, Caroline and Goodnow reached Beckley's home in Ann Arbor. The Beckley family was kind and welcoming. They wanted to hear Caroline's story and listened carefully as the girl told about her life in slavery.

With Guy Beckley's help, Caroline and Goodnow left for Detroit. They had food for the journey and directions to the home of Mr. and Mrs. Ambler. The Amblers' home was the last station on the Underground Railroad in Detroit. From their front door, Caroline could look across the Detroit River. On the other side, Canada was waiting.

Guy Beckley's house

12

One More River to Cross

It was nearly 6:00 in the evening when the tired horse pulled Caroline, Goodnow, and the buggy toward the Detroit River. The streets were crowded with workers hurrying home for supper. Boats floated along the riverfront. No one suspected that the young lady and middle-aged farmer jumping from the buggy in front of the Amblers' house were actually a fugitive slave and an abolitionist following the Underground Railroad. No one would have guessed they had traveled nearly 600 miles and been on the road for 3 weeks. No one would have thought they were still being chased, even in Detroit.

Goodnow knocked on the door. Mrs. Ambler answered and, in a blink, Caroline and Goodnow slipped inside the house. It was the last station before the Underground

Railroad reached Canada. This would be Caroline's last night in the United States.

What a strange, frightening situation. On one side of the river, the law said Caroline was still the property of Mr. Hall. On the other side of the river, she would be free. That night, she would cross the river.

The Amblers were experienced Underground Railroad workers. Although Mr. Ambler was gone, Mrs. Ambler knew exactly what to do. She sent a message to 2 friends who owned a boat. They could be trusted. Once the sun set, they would take Caroline and Goodnow across the river. They'd leave Caroline at the riverside town of Sandwich. Mrs. Ambler gave them directions to the house of a **missionary** who helped people running from slavery.

With darkness to hide them, Caroline and Goodnow climbed aboard the small boat. Goodnow paid the fare. That $2 fare was the only money he had been asked to pay by anyone during the entire trip from Wisconsin. Every meal

missionary (**mish** uh ner ee): someone who is sent by a church or religious group to teach that group's faith

83

and bed had been given to them at no cost. People on the Underground Railroad wanted to help. They knew what they were doing was right and important. They wouldn't take money for doing what was right.

Caroline watched as the small boat pulled away from Detroit. The boats and buildings along the riverfront looked familiar to her. On both sides of the

WHI ID 53060

Detroit River, 1855

river, long docks stretched into the water. Warehouses and people crowded the streets. Voices and the low sound of ships' horns echoed. Lights reflected on the water.

Nearly an hour passed—though it must have seemed like a week to Caroline—before they reached the opposite shore. The man pulled his boat toward a dock and tied it safely. Goodnow got out and turned to help Caroline.

Suddenly, Caroline clutched Goodnow's arm. She began to cry. "Are you taking me back?" she asked.

Goodnow didn't understand why she was crying. What was wrong?

Caroline cried out: "Is this St. Louis? Are you taking me back to St. Louis?" Panic and fear showed on her face. She must have been shaking.

Goodnow was shocked. Caroline thought he had betrayed her. She thought he was taking her back to St. Louis to collect the reward money.

He tried to explain. Of course he would never betray her. They were in Canada. The missionary's house was just steps away.

But Caroline said the river looked like the Mississippi River. Especially in the fading light, the shore looked familiar. Too familiar. The buildings and the docks looked like St. Louis. She cried and cried.

Goodnow tried to explain. He led Caroline toward the missionary's house. "You'll be safe," he assured her over and over. "This is Canada. The missionary will help you."

When they found the missionary's house, the pastor assured Caroline that she was safe. Goodnow said one, last, **bittersweet** good-bye and turned back to the dock where the boat was waiting.

Caroline watched him go. She called him "dearest friend." She watched and cried.

At that moment, a new part of Caroline's life began. She had traveled more than 1,000 miles. She'd been betrayed and chased. She'd met kind people and terrible people. She'd been afraid every hour of every day for nearly 3 months. Finally, she'd reached her dream. She had made it to Canada. It had cost her everything, but Caroline Quarlls had set herself free.

bittersweet (**bit** ur **sweet**): describes something that is happy and sad at the same time

13

Living Free and Going Home

What happened after Goodnow left Caroline at the mission house in Sandwich, Ontario, Canada? Goodnow returned to Detroit to hear some interesting news. A few hours earlier, that news would have been terrifying. Then, it was almost funny.

Goodnow discovered that he and Caroline had made a narrow escape. During the whole time Caroline and Goodnow had been traveling from Beebe's Grove back in Illinois, a clerk from the riverboat company in St. Louis had been waiting in Detroit. Once he finished putting up the reward posters, the clerk figured Caroline would pass through Detroit to reach Canada. So, he planted himself like a weed at the docks in Detroit. For 2 weeks, he'd been watching every ferryboat crossing to Canada. Every day, the clerk searched the crowds for Caroline's face. Night after night, he hid in the shadows, hoping to catch her.

But the clerk never saw Caroline. The ferryboat owner was an abolitionist. He crossed the river when and where the clerk wasn't watching. Goodnow knew Caroline was safe in Sandwich. The Amblers, the ferryboat owner, and the missionary could be trusted to keep her secret.

The clerk returned to St. Louis empty-handed. In the end, the riverboat owners had to pay $800 to Mr. Hall because they'd sold Caroline a ticket that Fourth of July evening.

Goodnow returned to Wisconsin. He still had crops to harvest and a farm to run. It took another 3 weeks to make the long return trip.

On the way back, Goodnow stopped at the little house outside Climax to pick up Caroline's bag containing the jewelry and money. He was in for a rude surprise. The man refused to give him Caroline's things. He gave one excuse after another. He said maybe Caroline would come later and ask for the jewelry and money. Then he'd be in trouble. He even hinted that maybe Goodnow couldn't be trusted.

Goodnow was ready to explode with frustration. He asked nicely at first. Then he tried to reason with the man. But the man wouldn't budge. Goodnow was convinced the man planned to keep the jewelry and money. What could he do?

Of course, Goodnow couldn't **threaten** the man. Finally, he remembered the letter Dr. Dyer had written back in Wisconsin. Maybe the letter would help. He headed off on foot to see Dr. Thayer, an abolitionist in a nearby town.

Dr. Thayer listened carefully. He read Dr. Dyer's letter. The idea that someone would try to cheat Caroline made him furious. He whipped out paper and pen and wrote a letter, demanding that Caroline's things be returned immediately.

Goodnow reached the man's house and pounded on the door. He pushed Dr. Thayer's letter into the man's hands. Now, would he return Caroline's belongings? At last, the man realized he had no choice. He handed over Caroline's bag with her precious jewelry and remaining money. In return, Goodnow told him exactly what he thought of someone so greedy that he'd cheat a young girl out of her only possessions.

threaten (**thret** uhn): to scare someone or put someone in danger

By the time Goodnow reached home, he'd been gone nearly 6 weeks—a month and a half. It was almost the end of September. Harvest was nearly over. Friends must have harvested his crops and cared for his animals.

COURTESY OF BURLINGTON HISTORICAL SOCIETY

Goodnow spent the rest of his life in Prairieville. Years later, when the town changed its name to Waukesha, he was known as one of the town's pioneers.

Lyman Goodnow as an older man

Almost 40 years later, Goodnow told what he knew of Caroline's story to historians writing the history of Milwaukee. He said:

> There you have the story of how the first passenger by the Underground Railroad traveled from Milwaukee to Canada. A great many went by the same route afterwards; and everyone arrived safely in

the land of freedom. I am now 81 years of age; but in all my long life I have done nothing that [gave me] more pleasure or of which I am more proud, than the part I took in freeing slaves.

While Goodnow returned to his life as a Wisconsin farmer, Caroline was making a whole new life for herself in Canada. She got a job and married. At some point, she learned to read and write.

In 1880, Goodnow wrote to Caroline. Her answer was filled with joy and surprise to hear from her old friend. In 2 separate letters, Caroline described her life in Canada. That life started, of course, as she stood crying in front of the missionary's house, watching her friend Goodnow walk away.

She stayed for some time with the missionary in the riverfront town of Sandwich. The missionary, Reverend Haskell, had been sent by his church to help people running from slavery. When people arrived with nothing but the clothes on their backs, Reverend Haskell made sure they received warm clothes. He helped people get jobs at farms

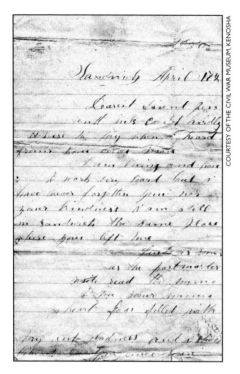

COURTESY OF THE CIVIL WAR MUSEUM, KENOSHA

**Letter from Caroline
to Lyman Goodnow**

COURTESY OF THE CIVIL WAR MUSEUM, KENOSHA

1880

Sandwich April 17th

Dearest friend, pen and ink could hardly express my joy when i heard from you once more.

I am living and have to work very hard but i have never forgotten you nor your kindness. i am still in Sandwich the same place where you left me.

Just as soon as the postmaster read to me, your name, my heart was filled with joy and gladness and i should like to see you once more Before i die to return you thanks for your kindness towards me.

I would like for you to send me one of those books that you was speaking about.

Dearest friend, you don't know how rejoiced i feel since i heard from you.

Answer this as soon as you get it and let me know how you are and your address.

Direct your letter to Caroline Watkins Sandwich, Ont. Ca 98

i hope you will send me one of those books you spoke of to the post master.

Caroline's letter to Lyman Goodnow is very old and difficult to read. Here is a copy of what she wrote.

and businesses. Sometimes, he helped them contact family still in slavery back in the United States.

Caroline needed work and a place to stay. She found both when she was hired on Colonel Prince's farm near Sandwich. Caroline was used to hard work. She knew how to sew, cook, and clean.

Caroline was relieved to have work and a place to live. But she wanted more. When missionaries started a school for **freedmen**, Caroline signed up. She'd learned some letters of the alphabet back in St. Louis, but she wanted to read and write.

A year or so later, Caroline met Allen Watkins, a man working on Colonel Prince's farm. Watkins had freed himself by running from slavery in Kentucky. As Caroline got to know him, she heard his story. She shared her story with him. They had both left loved ones and sad memories behind when they ran from slavery.

freedman: a person who had been a slave and bought, was given, or took his or her freedom

Caroline had left her grandmother and stepfather back in St. Louis. All her life, she carried sadness in her heart knowing that she left them behind.

Allen Watkins had left 3 children in Kentucky. He'd been married. When their 3 children were sold away from them, Allen Watkins and his wife were crushed and heartbroken. His wife lost all hope and took her own life. Everything he loved had been taken from him. So Watkins ran to Canada.

Caroline was much younger than Watkins. But in time they grew to love and care for each other. About 3 years after Caroline arrived in Canada, they married. She wasn't yet 20 years old. But a new part of her life had begun.

Together, Caroline and Allen had 6 children—3 girls and 3 boys. Watkins worked as a cook.

At this time, most children in Canada went to elementary school and then left school to work at their family's farm or business. But Caroline and Watkins wanted more for their children. They worked hard so that their children could have a good education. In 1880, Caroline wrote Goodnow that her oldest son owned his own farm. One son was a businessman in Ohio. Her youngest daughter was studying to teach school. Caroline was so proud.

Caroline's story was such an adventure. She risked everything to get freedom. It's easy to think that her life was good and easy after she risked her life, escaped slave hunters, and traveled 600 miles to freedom. But that wasn't what happened.

Caroline worked hard in Canada. She even wondered, as the years passed, if she had done the right thing by leaving her family and running away.

Although life wasn't easy or even always happy for Caroline, she and Allen raised a loving, close family in Sandwich. Some of their children emigrated to the United States. Some stayed, married, and raised their own families in Canada.

BURLINGTON HISTORICAL SOCIETY. PHOTO BY ROGER BINEMAN

Caroline's great-great-granddaughter, Charlotte Watkins, second from right, and her family

Today, members of Caroline and Allen's family still live in Sandwich in Ontario, Canada. Caroline's great-grandchildren and great-great-grandchildren still remember stories about her.

Caroline's great-great-granddaughter, Charlotte Watkins, remembers that Caroline made lace. She tells her own children and grandchildren that Caroline and Allen helped build a church in Sandwich. Later, they built a house that is still standing today. Charlotte says her granddaughter, Caroline's great-great-great-great-granddaughter, even looks a lot like Caroline!

The story of Caroline Quarlls started with a young girl longing to be free. But Caroline's story is more than an adventure. It's more than a tale of a brave girl and the brave people who helped her. It's a story of her dream and the cost of her freedom.

A Milwaukee mural on Fond du Lac Avenue tells the stories of prominent members of the Underground Railroad, including Caroline Quarlls.

Author's Note

A question I often hear when I visit schools and libraries is, "Where did you find this story from history?" I usually answer, "Stories are written in old newspapers, letters, diaries, pictures, maps, and books." Finding stories like Caroline's is like digging for treasure, except you dig in libraries and historical society **"rare book" rooms**.

Many different people wrote about Caroline in many different places. A letter, book, newspaper, or other place where information is written is called a *source*. In all, *12* sources were used to put together all the puzzle pieces of Caroline's story.

Different people remembered and wrote down different information. For example, we know about Caroline's clothes because Samuel and Lucinda Daugherty's daughter, Almira Daughtery Woodruff, wrote about them in a book called *The History of Waukesha County*. Here is what she wrote:

rare book room: a place where unique and valuable books are kept

My sister Anne said she had an elegant dress that she had to suddenly hide in the barrel without changing, and also…jewelry in a handbag. The dress was silk grenadine and it was torn nearly from her by bushes in the dark.

I feel grateful to all the women and men living so long ago who remembered and wrote about Caroline's brave, risky adventure. Without them I would never have shared Caroline's frightening experience in the sugar barrel. I wouldn't have understood how determined the slave hunters were to catch her or how many people helped Caroline hide and escape. Without those people, I wouldn't have discovered Caroline's amazing, powerful story. And, without those people, I wouldn't have been able to share that story with you today.

Glossary

abolitionist (ab uh **lish** uh nist): a person who is against slavery

bachelor (**bach** uh lur): an unmarried man

betrayed (bee **trayd**): turned against someone, especially in a time of need

bittersweet (**bit** ur **sweet**): describes something that is happy and sad at the same time

blacksmith: someone who makes and fits horseshoes and mends things made of iron

bounty hunter (**boun** tee **huhnt** ur): a person who caught runaway slaves for money

by-and-by (**bye** and **bye**): later, after some time has passed

campaign (kam **payn**): a series of actions organized to win something, such as a political election

chute (**shoot**): a narrow, tilted passage for goods, garbage, laundry, grain, or coal

fanatic (fuh **nat** ik): a person who is very excited about a belief, cause, or interest

freedman: a person who had been a slave and bought, was given, or took his or her freedom

fugitive (fyoo juh tiv): someone who is running away, especially from the police

harbor (har bur): a place where boats stop or unload their goods

harboring (har bur ing): hiding someone

hogshead (hogz hed): type of wood or heavy pottery barrel that holds about 60 gallons

ladies' seminary (se meh ner ee): a school where girls were taught to be proper ladies

missionary (mish uh ner ee): someone who is sent by a church or religious group to teach that group's faith

posse (poss ee): a group of people gathered together to help catch a criminal

preacher (preech ur): a person who gives a religious talk to people, especially during a church service

pursued (per **sood**): chased or followed by someone

pursuer (per **soo** er): a person chasing someone in order to catch him or her

rare book room: a place where unique and valuable books are kept

rickety (rik uh tee): old, weak, and likely to break

spied (spyed): sighted

sued (sood): started a case against someone in a court of law

thee: an old word for you

threaten (**thret** uhn): to scare someone or put someone in danger

toting (**toht** ing): carrying or hauling something

traitor (**tray** tur): a person who is false to a friend, cause, or trust

warrant (**wor** uhnt): a legal paper that gives permission for something, like to search property or to arrest a person

will: written instructions that tell what should be done with someone's property and money when that person dies

Reading Group Guide and Activities

Discussion Questions

❧ In her letter to Lyman Goodnow, Caroline wrote that she was kept as a slave to do housework. She wrote that she had been beaten but otherwise was treated "well enough." If Mr. and Mrs. Hall, Caroline's owners, had treated her with kindness instead of beating her, would that have made owning a slave any different? Why or why not?

❧ Caroline wrote that she wasn't very happy after escaping to Canada. She said she wondered if she had done the right thing by running away. Why do you think she felt this way?

❧ Robert Titball was a black man who said he had once been a slave. Were you surprised when you read that he betrayed Caroline and tried to turn her over to slave hunters? Why or why not?

❧ People escaping from slavery and people involved in the Underground Railroad all took risks. Sometimes people's lives were in danger. Sometimes they risked being put in jail. People running away always risked being caught and returned to slavery. Find 3 events where someone took a risk during Caroline's journey to freedom. What harm could have come to that person?

❖ What person in this story seemed the most unusual or interesting to you? Why?

❖ Caroline ran away without knowing where she was going or what she would do when she got to a free place. What did she do that seems clever or smart? What did she do that seems risky and dangerous?

Activities

❖ Create a map of the Midwest and include Missouri, Illinois, Wisconsin, Indiana, Michigan, the Great Lakes, the western shore of Ontario, Canada, and any bordering states. Make a list of every place Caroline traveled. Draw a line showing her journey on the map.

❖ Illustrate one event in Caroline's story. Choose any medium. Examples may include drawing, shoe box exhibits, collage, painting, or even photos taken of someone re-creating the event.

❖ Write Caroline's story from the point of view of different people involved. You'll want to include Caroline, Mr. Hall, Robert Titball, Asahel Finch, Matthew Spencer, Lucinda Daugherty, and Lyman Goodnow. "Assemble" the whole story by writing each person's contributions and thoughts on a poster along with an illustration of one event in which that person was involved. Perhaps the whole story could be "told" by hanging your posters in the school hallway.

To Learn More about Caroline Quarlls and the Underground Railroad

Blockson, Charles. *The Underground Railroad*. New York: Berkeley Books, 1987.

Hamilton, Virginia. *Many Thousand Gone*. New York: Knopf Publishers, 1993.

The History of Waukesha County. Chicago: Western Historical Company, 1880.

Hurmence, Berlinda. *Slavery Time When I Was Chillun'*. New York: Putnam Publishers, 1997.

Lester, Julius. *From Slave Ship to Freedom Road*. New York: Puffin Books, 1998.

Pferdehirt, Julia. *Freedom Train North: Stories of the Underground Railroad in Wisconsin*. Middleton, WI: Living History Press, 1998.

You'll find information about Caroline Quarlls, including copies of Lyman Goodnow's words from *The History of Waukesha County* and Caroline's letters to Goodnow, at Julia Pferdehirt's Web site: www.teachingwithstories.com.

Acknowledgments

My thanks to Peg and Thomas Kilpatrick of Waukesha for so generously sharing Caroline's letters. And thanks to Charlotte Watkins for sharing family stories from the freedom side of Caroline's journey.

Index

This index points you to the pages where you can read about persons, places, and ideas. If you do not find the word you are looking for, try to think of another word that means about the same thing.

When you see a page number in **bold** it means there is a picture on that page.